ARE
WE
LIVE?

ARE WE LIVE?

THE FUNNIEST BLOOPERS FROM TV AND RADIO

Marion Appleby

Michael O'Mara Books Limited

First published in Great Britain in 2012 by
Michael O'Mara Books Limited
9 Lion Yard
Tremadoc Road
London SW4 7NQ

A CIP catalogue record for this book is available from the
British Library.

Papers used by Michael O'Mara Books Limited are natural,
recyclable products made from wood grown in sustainable
forests. The manufacturing processes conform to the
environmental regulations of the country of origin.

ISBN: 978-1-84317-866-8 in paperback print format
ISBN: 978-1-84317-963-4 in EPub format
ISBN: 978-1-84317-964-1 in Mobipocket format

1 2 3 4 5 6 7 8 9 10

Cover design by Ana Bjezancevic

Designed and typeset by K.DESIGN, Somerset

Illustrations by Andrew Pinder

Printed and bound by CPI Group (UK) Ltd,
Croydon, CR0 4YY

www.mombooks.com

CONTENTS

INTRODUCTION

BRACE YOURSELF

In the live studio environment, anything can happen. This is why production companies rely on rigorously edited scripts, bossy floor managers and teams of runners to attend to a TV star's every unreasonable whim. But all the meetings in the world cannot control that most uncontrollable of things: the human spirit. We humans do not speak according to schedule, we do not always flip the right switch, and sometimes we get angry. Very, very angry. Angry enough, even, to pull out a gun during the news.

Are We Live? is a book about all the things that can, and have, gone wrong on television and radio. It's about fluffing the autocue, swearing at audiences and saying no when your boyfriend proposes to you in the middle of a televised baseball game. It's about ringing into a Saturday-morning children's television show and calling yourself Jenny Tailia. It's also about taking off all of your clothes and running across a cricket pitch, waving your pants in triumph. It's about animals pooping and pecking; life and its very unpredictability.

This book is divided into handy sections, with not a misplaced word nor an accidental profanity littering its pages. It's serious too, with important information for all public figures on How to Remember When Your Mic Is Still On. There are also heroes, like the amiable Guy Goma – the man who went for an interview in the accounts department of the BBC only to find himself on a rolling-news broadcast facing questions about illegal downloading. His horrified face should truly be a lesson to us all.

There are also rude bits; the bits some celebrities show us when they suffer accidental wardrobe malfunctions. Judy Finnigan, Nicki Minaj, lady newsreader with the too-short skirt: you have not exposed yourselves in vain. We remember you; we enjoyed your undeliberate flashes of boob and knicker.

Are We Live? attempts to answer the most difficult of questions: Why would anyone agree to appear on live television? And who in their right mind would present a weather bulletin when standing next to a massive pelican?

BAD ROMANCE

ROMANTIC MISFIRES

Even the most jaded of souls likes a bit of romance in their life. But one thing's for sure – a live broadcast is not the way to woo a potential partner, propose to your current squeeze or indeed call to an end a dying relationship. Especially if you both happen to be very famous.

A Match Made In Heaven

There's nothing like a story of a nice engagement to warm the heart. Although the same can't be said for this story . . .

Actually, I don't think I do

If live television teaches us anything it is: DO NOT USE IT TO PROPOSE TO YOUR PARTNER. For every one hundred accepted proposals, there are three angry 'What?' responses. And nobody, not even you, wants to be on the receiving end of one of those three.

Host #1: We've got a little surprise for you out there in TV land, and here in the studio audience. Nobody knows what's going on next.

Host #2: I want to do something kind of special. This was not scripted, this was not a plan. Nobody knows this is about to happen. So not only are you watching this at home for the first time, all the people in the audience are watching it for the first time too. So, is there a Mike in the audience? Everybody give a nice round of applause for Mike!

Mike: Yeah, um, I've been with my girlfriend Lynne for a few months now. Best months of my life. And ah, it's the season, so I wanted to ask her . . . Lynne, ah, it's been the happiest months of my life and I wanted to ask you to marry me.

Lynne: Can we talk about this later? [ETERNITY-LENGTH PAUSE] . . . Can we?

Host#1: Ah, we'll be right back. Ah, awkward.

The Almost Late Show with Bobby Bones

URBAN LEGENDS
The myths of live broadcast debunked

On Valentine's Day 2007, student Ryan Burke filmed himself breaking-up with his girlfriend in front of a crowd of hundreds. The very public performance included Burke shouting, 'Look, I fucking know you fucked Brad. Like, seriously, how the fuck can you do that to somebody that you care about?'

Dumbfounded, Burke's baffled girlfriend replied, 'You seriously bought these fucking people to do this? ... You really want to air this all out?' She then went on to say some rather embarrassing things about how, as a woman, she had 'needs' that weren't exactly being catered for, accusing Burke of being gay.

Two weeks later, Fox News interviewed Burke, who admitted the stunt had been a hoax designed to demonstrate the 'power of the Internet', and to help promote his new music PR company.

Let's Call It a Day

Breaking up is hard to do. Especially if it's in front of an audience of millions . . .

On second thoughts

In 2009, Jason Mesnick, star of the US hit television show *The Bachelor*, broke off his engagement to female contestant Melissa Rycroft live on television.

After an engagement of six whole weeks, Mesnick chose the season finale to tell Rycroft that he sort of preferred the show's runner-up contestant, Molly. Upon hearing the news, a clearly distraught Rycroft said (in a strange use of the third person), 'So, you told Melissa you loved her, you put a ring on Melissa's finger, but you don't want to fight for Melissa.' She then, quite rightly, called him a bastard.

'Watching television is like taking black
spray paint to your third eye.' BILL HICKS

URBAN LEGENDS
The myths of live broadcast debunked

The story goes that Matt Damon broke up with his *Good Will Hunting* co-star Minnie Driver live on television's *The Oprah Winfrey Show* in front of an audience of millions.

However, despite Damon's revelations, he and Driver had in fact broken up a week or so previously. Although it's fair to say Driver was rather unimpressed with Damon talking about the split, especially as it was with one of America's most popular television show hosts. Driver later told *The Times*, 'It's unfortunate that Matt went on *Oprah*. It seemed like a good forum for him to announce to the world that we were no longer together, which I found fantastically inappropriate.'

Not cool

After finding out his girlfriend of five years, Ashley, had been caught cheating on him, Chris enlisted the help of radio DJs Woody and Rizzuto to dump her live on air. Having duped Ashley into thinking he was going to propose to her, Chris told her, 'We've been together for five years now and I've loved you with all of my heart and dreamed of spending the rest of my life with you ... I guess I just have one thing to ask you ... How long will it take you to get your crap out of my house?'

However, despite Woody and Rizzuto's protestations to the contrary, the whole thing's got to have been a set-up. The excruciating broadcast is a whole ten minutes long and ends with Ashley in tears and the radio DJs in fits of giggles – it's got to be a fake. Or has it ...?

How Insulting!

Men of the world take heed: hell hath no fury like a woman scorned. Or certainly one with a microphone in her hand.

Walls have ears

In June 2000, viewers of Channel Ten Brisbane's news bulletin gained an insight into newsreader Mary Louise Thielle's life when she referred to her husband as 'this arsehole I'm married to' live on air.

Thinking they were still on a commercial break, Thielle can be heard chatting to her fellow news anchor about him indoors. She apologized the following day.

'I find television to be very educating. Every time somebody turns on the set, I go in the other room and read a book.'

GROUCHO MARX

URBAN LEGENDS
The myths of live broadcast debunked

Chris Taylor, a guest on popular Australian breakfast television show *Sunrise*, chose his chance in the limelight to announce directly to camera, 'My partner, Jo, never misses the show . . . so can I just put a message out to her? We've been together for seven years, and I just want to take this opportunity now live on television to say, Jo, get the fuck out of my life!'

However, despite realistic onscreen graphics and some pretty good acting from the show's real presenters, Taylor later confessed that the whole thing had been a set-up. It was in fact part of an elaborate series of pranks for Australian comedy series *The Chaser's War on Everything*.

> 'Television: teacher, mother, secret lover.'
>
> HOMER SIMPSON

Is *that* it?

During a sports report on Australia's *Ten News at Five*, news anchor Belinda Heggen delivered a low blow when she mocked the size of her co-anchor's manhood.

After footage was shown of English cricketer Andrew Strauss proudly showing off what looked to be the world's smallest trophy, co-anchor Mark Aiston said, 'Belinda, I just can't understand how something so small can be so impressive.' To which she replied,

'Well, Mark, you would know about that.' She gamely carried on presenting, while Mark no doubt wept inside.

'Television: chewing gum for the eyes.'
ARCHITECT FRANK LLOYD WRIGHT

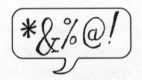

BODILY DYSFUNCTION

LETTING LOOSE

When you're in a tense situation, sometimes your brain goes into anxiety mode: *What if my hand does that funny, flappy thing? What if my leg won't stop jigging up and down? Oh, God, OH, GOD, what if I fart?* Make no mistake – this is not idle paranoia. People really do fart on live television. And throw up. And sometimes they even wee. But that's mostly the animals.

The Demon Drink

Two things it's best not to combine: copious amounts of alcohol and live television. It will only end in disaster.

Propped up

'[While] doing a piece to camera on the Greek island where *Shirley Valentine* was filmed ... we grabbed a bottle of retsina as a prop and off we went. The only problem was that each take was spoiled by something ... But each time I had already taken a slug of retsina needed for the shot. Eventually, it was just me cocking up. I had to be helped off the beach.'

Former *GMTV* breakfast show host Penny Smith
on the perils of drinking on camera

'If it weren't for the fact that the TV set and refrigerator are so far apart, some of us wouldn't get any exercise at all.'

COMEDIAN JOEY ADAMS

In denial

Reality TV show *The Club* – in which three celebrities were each given control of a bar in a London club – aired in the UK in 2003 for just six weeks. In that short time it still provided us with one of TV's most uncomfortable moments: a clearly drunk veteran glamour model Samantha Fox (who also happened to be dressed up as a vampire) vehemently denying her state of intoxication during a live interview with her on-screen employee Steve.

Wide-eyed and slurring her words, Fox's defence to the accusation that she was drunk was that she's an actress playing the part of a drunk – 'I don't need to be drunk to be like this. I'm like this at nine a clock in the morning!' Just a few moments later she called Steve 'an arsehole' and claimed, 'I don't even drink.' Her clearly incensed employee then proclaimed, '[You] lying cow ... I've served you drinks!' Despite Steve's trump card, Fox still managed to grab the last word to Steve: 'It's a shame about your little knob, innit?'

URBAN LEGENDS

The myths of live broadcast debunked

Erik Hartman, the host of a Flemish daytime talk show, was once unable to continue interviewing his guests due to a massive fit of the giggles during a discussion on 'medical mistakes'. Hartman's laughing fit appeared to have been provoked by two vocally challenged guests: the first of whom had an incredibly high-pitched voice caused by a recent, botched tonsillectomy; the second of whom sported a low, robotic voice due to his use of an electronic speech device that had been fitted after a laryngectomy.

However, despite over 10 million hits on YouTube and an outing on *The Tonight Show with Jay Leno*, the chat show was in fact faked. The sketch had been created for satirical sketch show *In De Gloria*, and the corpsing talk show host was actually played by comedian and actor Tom Van Dyck.

Zip It!

Everything could be going smoothly – the autocue's working perfectly, the guests have been a dream ... but then the uncontrollable happens: your wardrobe malfunctions.

'Time has convinced me of one thing: television is for appearing on, not looking at.'   NOËL COWARD

Prize-winning idiot

Former hosts of ITV's flagship daytime television show *This Morning*, Richard Madeley and Judy Finnigan, managed an amazing wardrobe fail in 2000 when they collected the award for Most Popular Daytime Programme at the National Television Awards.

The problem began when Judy ascended the podium with her dress half-mast, leaving her well-upholstered breasts on show. Taking their statuettes from presenter Les Dennis, the couple turned to face the front, whereupon a full view of Finnigan's bra was finally exposed, to mounting cries from the audience. Sadly, Madeley mistook the hoots and squeals for requests for him to perform his (substandard) Ali G impression. It makes for an unbearable watch.

Here's how it went down:

Richard: No, I'm not doing it, I'm not doing it.

Judy: [Adjusting her jacket – she's clearly feeling a bit chilly, but doesn't yet realize why.] The real one's [Ali G] here!

[Audience roars, at which point someone races up to the podium to adjust Judy's top. Both she and Richard then realize their mistake.]

Judy: Ohhhh!

Richard: It's OK, they'll cut it out! They'll never show it!

Judy: It's live!

Avert your eyes

Rapper Nicki Minaj suffered an embarrassing wardrobe malfunction while performing live on *Good Morning America*. During a lively performance of her latest single, Minaj accidentally exposed her left nipple. Despite the recording's five-second delay, Nicki's bits were broadcast to the entire nation. Oops!

No Funny Business

Sex, sex, sex: it makes the world go round. Even live
TV can't seem to get enough of it!

Is that a wad of cash in your pocket?

Male anchor: And we've the latest on the Labour
  MP thrown out of Parliament after fiddling her
  erection expenses. [Notices female anchor
  staring at him.] Did I say erection? I did, didn't I?

BBC *Look North*

Location, location, location

In 1977, Bob Eubanks, the host of *The Newlywed Game*, posed a slightly risqué question to a young couple that garnered an even more risqué response.

Bob: Here's the last of our five-point questions: Tell me where, specifically, is the *weirdest* place that you have ever gotten the urge to make whoopee [have sex]. Olga?

Olga: [Giggling.] In the ass?

[Slight pause, whole studio erupts in laughter.]

Bob: No, no, no. What I'm talking about is the weirdest *location*.

Olga: The weirdest location. I don't know.

Bob: Give me an answer, please. He [Olga's husband] said it was in the car, on the freeway.

Olga: [Cringes silently.]

Cheap joke

Celebrity chef Ainsley Harriott trades in on his West Indian heritage.

Ainsley Harriott: Those Glamorgan sausages are a little bit on the black side, are they not? You're prepared to try it, are you?

Contestant: Yup, yup.

Ainsley Harriott: Ooh, that's always good, I like a girl who likes a black sausage [raises eyebrow at camera].

Can't Cook, Won't Cook, BBC One

Pooooeeeee!

It's hard to maintain your decorum when faced with a nasty honk – especially if you're live on television. Just thank the Lord smell-o-vision hasn't been invented yet!

'[Television is] an invention that permits you to be entertained in your living room by people you wouldn't have in your home.'

VETERAN BROADCASTER DAVID FROST

An assault on the senses

Pregnant newscaster Kate Silverton nearly vomited during an interview with British comedian David Walliams during an interview on the BBC's News 24 channel in 2011.

Presented with Walliams's scratch-and-sniff booklet, Silverton took a good whiff of a panel that was meant to smell like 'two pairs of moldy socks, one dirty nappy, three rancid tins of tuna, some rotting carpet, an old cabbage and a small pile of cat poo'. While a graphic of the offending page was shown on screen, Silverton could be heard retching very loudly, exclaiming, 'Oh, that's exactly what I thought it would smell like!'

Skip the bran flakes!

Californian weatherman Aaron Perlman felt the need to explain to viewers why he was unable to deliver the weather bulletin without giggling. Welcoming back the audience after the commercial break, Perlman quickly lost it, saying, 'In all my years as a weatherman I have never come out of a commercial break laughing so hard. Sorry.' But his colleagues on the news desk wouldn't rest until he revealed exactly why he was laughing. 'Aaron had a bodily function error just after the break,' said one co-anchor. 'Let's just say the winds picked up pretty strong in here . . . I think you know what we mean.'

Perlman attempted to seize back control by continuing to deliver the bulletin, with, 'The winds coming out of the south are bringing cloudy skies for the rest of the day.' His co-host quipped, 'The winds did come out of the south.' Exasperated and close to collapse, Perlman eventually came clean, 'Don't tell me that you guys don't fart!'

URBAN LEGENDS

The myths of live broadcast debunked

'Ambush', the live episode of popular US medical drama *ER*, was thought to show George Clooney picking his nose.

However, although the episode was performed live twice (for the benefit of east- and west-coast US audiences), the only mistakes made included one actor losing his weapon and another actor dropping his pen. Clooney wasn't even in it!

Parp Idol

Chelsea Johnson gave more than she bargained for when she auditioned for *Canadian Idol*. After composing herself in front of the judges, ready to belt out her song, poor Chelsea belted out instead a languorous fart. 'I totally just farted!' exclaimed the stricken contestant.

Animal Magic

Never work with animals. Especially on live TV. There's no predicting what they might do.

Urgent matters

In 2012, at the prestigious UK annual dog competition Crufts, a dog, who just happened to be making excellent time on his run, stopped to take a poo. The whole thing was caught on camera, and the dog was immediately disqualified.

Skinny cow!

California's KMAX-TV anchor Mark Allen got more than he bargained for when he reported live from the Dixon May Fair in 2008. As he started to deliver his entertainment report, the poor presenter didn't realize that one of the two cows standing directly behind him had decided to take a lengthy poo. 'What is your secret?' Allen asked the cow. 'I've been doing [the] South Beach [diet] and I haven't had that kind of action for weeks!'

'Television is more interesting than people. If it were not, we should have people standing in the corners of our rooms.'

ALAN COREN

Interrupted flow

Reporting on a dog-shooting incident in Toledo, ABC news reporter Tony Geftos was cradling a 3-foot-long alligator – also found at the scene – in his arms when the miscreant reptile decided to take a leak. The urine could be seen trickling down poor Geftos's arm, as he ably continued with his report.

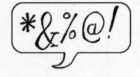

NOT IN FRONT OF THE CHILDREN

CLOSE YOUR EARS

Kids' television is a high-octane assault on the senses, full of throbbing lights, lots of noise and daft skits. But what happens when you invite that really cool band to come on and play their slightly risqué new song? Or when a naughty little cherub decides to call into the morning phone-in and shout obscenities down the line . . .?

Having a Pop

Endless rounds of press junkets when they've got a new single to promote can mean pop groups are often overexposed. So you can perhaps forgive the foul-mouthed few who've let rip at the latest boy band live on air.

Charming!

In 1984, a naughty man called Simon Roberts decided to use the forum of a Saturday-morning children's television programme to tell eighties pop group Matt Bianco exactly what he thought of them.

Mike Read: Simon Roberts on the line. Hello, Simon.

Simon Roberts: Hello.

Mike Read: You're through to Matt Bianco.

Simon Roberts: Hello, Matt Bianco.

Matt Bianco: Hello!

Simon Roberts: You're a bunch of wankers.

[Sound of dial tone.]

Mike Read: Hello. . .? He's gone.

Saturday Superstore, BBC One

EXPLOSIVE TELEVISION!

In 1989, squeaky-clean TV presenter Anthea Turner was seriously injured when pyrotechnics exploded in her face live on Saturday-morning children's television program *UP2U*.

Presenting a piece to camera from the back of a truck, a very young Turner can be seen grinning and swinging her legs before a motorcycle stuntman emerges from the vehicle and a huge explosion propels her to the ground. In a darkly ironic twist, Turner's last words before the blast were, 'If you want something to happen to you ...' Unfortunately, the poor lady was left with some quite serious burns and temporary hearing loss, and ended up suing the BBC.

'Today, watching television often means fighting, violence and foul language – and that's just deciding who gets to hold the remote control.'

CHILDREN'S AUTHOR DONNA GEPHART

Why I oughta . . .

Naughty Eliot Fletcher decided to give pop group Five Star a piece of his mind when he called into kids' TV show *Going Live!* in 1989.

Sarah Greene: OK, Eliot, what's your question?

Eliot Fletcher: I'd like to ask Five Star why they're so fucking crap! They're fucking mother— [cut off]

Sarah Greene: Thanks very much, Eliot! Nice to hear from you. Let's move on to line three. Have you got a sensible question?

Going Live!, BBC One

Do As I Do

Sometimes it's the celebrities themselves that forget where they are and utter words that shouldn't see the light of day on children's TV.

Boomtown brat

In 2003, in a segment in which celebrity guests review the latest singles on ITV's Saturday-morning children's show *CD:UK*, guest, serial-swearer Bob Geldof, let it all hang out.

He started fairly tamely by professing his enthusiasm for Irish band the Thrills. After a video of their new single 'Don't Steal Our Sun' had run, Geldof told presenter Cat Deeley, 'They're a proper band, aren't they, there's no sort of dicking around.' Clearly warming to his theme, Geldof wouldn't take no for an answer when it turned out there wasn't enough time left to show the final single. 'Do it anyway,' he told Deeley. 'Fuck the tape! Come on!'

Icky Pop

Iggy Pop once appeared on ITV's live Saturday-morning children's television programme *No. 73*, performing the song 'Wild One' as he simulated sex with a giant teddy bear.

Although Iggy somewhat heroically managed to keep his top on for the whole of the performance, he did simulate sexy times with a teddy bear, thrusting the stuffed toy's bottom to the general area of his own crotch. Iggy reportedly found it 'quite difficult' to secure bookings on British television for 'some time' thereafter.

Jedward ~~are~~ say shit

In November 2009, *X Factor* UK rejects twins John and Edward Grimes made an inauspicious debut on RTÉ's ever-popular *The Late Late Show* spin-off, *Toy Show*. Keen to show off his talents, an excitable John decided to walk on his hands and do the splits at the same time . . . with the inevitable result to his trouser gusset. 'Oh, shit,' said the tower-haired pop star. 'I've ripped my pants. Oh, my God, that was not planned.' Luckily the show aired post-watershed at 11pm.

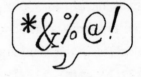

RADIO GA-GA

MAKING WAVES

Many of us might think of radio as a genteel world, home to veteran presenters, afternoon plays and competition phone-ins. But as the following tales will attest, exhausted hosts, nutty members of the public and clueless politicians have made for some radio-mishap gold!

Too Much Time on Their Hands

Imagine the scene: you're fifteen, you have no money and you're really, *really* bored. You're sitting in the kitchen with your best friend while a terrible local radio station plays in the background. Suddenly, you get an idea – what if you rang the station for a dedication and called yourself by a funny name?

I. P. Freely

'OK, let's get to our first dedication: "Dear Chris, please say a big hello to Connie Lingus, who's sixty-nine on Tuesday. She'll be enjoying my meat and two veg on Sunday at twelve. Wish her all the very best and tell her I look forward to seeing her when she comes." And that comes from Ivan Ardon.'

BBC Radio Leicestershire, April 2006

For inspiration, here's a list of the most popular names used during prank calls:

Harry Balls	Ben Dover	Mo Lestor
Gaye Barr	Al Fresco	Holden MacGroyne
Mr Bates	Willie B. Hardigan	Anita Mann
Harry Beard	Dick Hertz	Phil McCracken
Harry Beaver	Pat Hiscock	Monica Moorehead
Dick Bender	Mike Hunt	Bea O'Problem
Dick Burns	Dick Hunter	Fanny O'Rear
Seymour Bush	Buster Hymann	Ivan Oder
Seymour Butz	Heywood Jablome	Mike Rotch
Buster Cherry	Hugh Jass	Emma Royds
Harry Cox	Hugh Jorgan	Tess Steckle
I. P. Daly	Jack Knoff	Willie Stroker
Al Dente	Anita Lay	Dick Swett
Anita Dick	Willie Leak	Jenny Tull

Palin for all to see

It's not always the listeners who like to pull pranks. Canadian radio duo The Masked Avengers (or *Les Justiciers Masqués*), Sébastien Trudel and Marc-Antoine Audette, pulled a spectacular joke on Sarah Palin in November 2008. Posing as the then French President Nicolas Sarkozy, the pair managed to keep Palin on the line for almost six minutes.

The Masked Avengers managed to dupe a giddy-sounding Palin into believing French crooner Johnny Hallyday was Sarkozy's Special American Advisor and French Canadian country singer Stef Carse was the Prime Minister of Canada. The highlight, however, had to be their announcement that Sarkozy's wife Carla Bruni had written a song for Palin called '*Du rouge à lèvres sur un cochon*' (translation: 'Lipstick on a Pig').

Losing Their Cool

A handsome salary, countless freebies and free entry to glamorous parties are just some of the perks of being a DJ. But sometimes those early starts can play havoc with one's decorum.

'... And the last word today – Enoch Powell: the best prime minister we probably never had.'

Former BBC Radio 2 DJ Sarah Kennedy, airing her somewhat misguided support for Britain's most famous opponent of immigration

'It's the Queen Mum's birthday today. Ah, she smells of wee but we all love her.'

BBC Radio 1 DJ Sara Cox,
broadcasting live from Ibiza

'Hurry up, folks, and deposit your letters now. We'll be waiting for your droppings in the box.'

A radio announcer encourages listeners
to write in to the show

Finger pointing

BBC Radio 2 host Dermot O'Leary made a bit of a blunder when he insinuated his fellow host Sarah Kennedy had a problem with drink. When Alan Carr told O'Leary that he prefers to drink vodka because it can't be detected on his breath, O'Leary quipped, 'The Sarah Kennedy get-out.'

Setting the tempo

American radio host and popular personality Casey Kasem is best known for hosting the *American Top 40* show. But he's also quite famous for his radio rants, and not least for his most famous blow-up, which happened when he was trying to record a dedication for a listener's dead dog.

In a rant of ever-increasing ire, Kasem lambasted his producers for failing to provide appropriate music to lead into the sad story. He finished his piece with the following summary of his thoughts: 'I want somebody to use HIS FUCKING BRAIN to not come out of A GOD-DAMN RECORD that is up-tempo when I've got to talk about a FUCKING DOG DYING!' No doubt that was them told.

'98 per cent of American homes have TV sets, which means the people in the other 2 per cent have to generate their own sex and violence.' COMEDIAN GENE BAYLER

Please don't leave a message

In October 2008, tousle-haired lothario Russell Brand and his BBC Radio 2 co-host Jonathan Ross got themselves – and quite a few other members of BBC staff – into lots of trouble when they broadcast a series of naughty messages they'd left on actor Andrew Sachs's answerphone.

The pair originally called the actor to interview him for their show, but, when he failed to answer, Ross decided instead to tell Sachs's machine that Brand had 'fucked [his] granddaughter'. Brand followed with the equally regrettable, 'It was consensual and she wasn't menstrual.' Silly, silly boys.

The Audience Has It

'Actives' is an industry term for radio listeners who contact shows to request songs, participate in debates, or just to have a chat with the DJ. But perhaps it's time to coin a new phrase, 'bad actives', to describe a DJ's worst nightmare – the uncontrollable, mad or really stupid guest.

Bright spark

This caller to an Australian radio station – that was running a competition to win a motorbike to celebrate the release of a new AC/DC album – wasn't the sharpest tool in the box.

DJ #1: Hello. What's your name?

Caller: Mark!

DJ #1: Now, listen, Mark, do you like AC/DC?

Mark: Yeeeees.

DJ #1: And, do you have a motorcycle licence?

Mark: No. But I'll get one if I win it! I'm gonna win it.

DJ #1: Good, good. I like that confidence. Well, look, I have to ask you a question before I put your name in the draw.

Mark: OK . . .

DJ #1: Mark, spell 'AC/DC'.

Mark: AD . . . AC.

DJ #1: Um, I'm going to ask you again. How do you spell 'AC/DC'?

Mark: A . . . D . . . AC!

DJ #1: Mark, I'll kill you in a minute.

DJ #2: Mark. One more time. How do you spell 'AC/DC'?

[Silence.]

DJ #1: SPELL 'AC/DC'!

Mark: How to spell . . . A . . . D . . . D . . . C?

[Sound of giggling.]

Mark: A ... AD ... A ... I'm getting this all wrong!

DJ #1: Mark, you're getting it *seriously* wrong. JUST SPELL 'AC/DC'!

Mark: AD/DC!

DJ #1: AAAAAAARGH, YOU IDIOT, IT'S AC/DC!

Mark: AD/DC.

DJ #1: LOOK. A ... C ... D ... C. Just. Say. That.

Mark: AC/DC.

DJ #1 & 2: YEEEEEAAAASSSS!

DJ #1: Mark, it wasn't that hard!

DJ #2: OK, Mark, we're gonna give you a copy of your favourite AC/DC album. Do you have a favourite album?

Mark: Uhhhh, anything by AD/DC is good.

[Sound of DJs in fits of giggles.]

Mark: Oh, I'll get it right one of these days!

Triple M Radio, Australia

A piece of his mind

In September 2011, irate radio listener Jonathan from Swansea called in to talkSPORT to tell late-night DJ Matt Forde exactly what he – and, according to his estimates, 99 per cent of the station's listeners – thought of him.

During a seven-minute rant, Jonathan accused Matt of the following:

- 'You are a talentless liar, a shameless sycophantic sell-out with a jelly spine and a mush mind.'

- 'You even lied about being mugged just to gain sympathy.'

- 'You hate Western civilization.'

- 'You're the reason why we had the [UK summer 2011] riots.'

Matt held his own and, amidst hysterical giggles, managed to muster the following golden comeback: 'Jonathan, you've swallowed the Internet!'

Straight to the point

During a phone-in to discuss the issue of obesity, Radio 2's Jeremy Vine unwittingly pitched size-eighteen Alison against straight-talking Steve. After Jeremy asked, 'Is it time to stigmatize being fat?' the following exchange took place:

Steve: It's galling when people are travelling on low-cost airlines and you're in a queue with an enormously obese person who, God forbid, you're sitting next to.

Alison: I cannot believe that I'm hearing this.

Steve: You don't want to hear it because you're overweight and you're selfish.

Long live the republic

April 2011's Royal Wedding extravaganza between handsome Prince William and bonny Catherine Middleton drew in crowds from across the globe ... apart from poor Melvin from Milton Keynes. He wasn't very happy about the nuptials. Not very happy at all.

During a call to Jonathan Vernon-Smith's show on the UK's Three Counties Radio, Melvin professed the following:

- 'I feel like I wanna kill myself. I am so sick of it. I mean, what is the point?'

- 'It's going to be like the night of the living dead. All the zombie-like creatures coming out, going, "OooooOOOOoo! Lovely Royal Wedding!"'

As if to hammer home his dissatisfaction, Melvin finished with, 'Royal Wedding, Royal Wedding, ROYAL WEDDING. I tell you, I'm bloody FED UP!' before hanging up.

'There's too much nudity on TV, and not enough on the radio.'

AUTHOR JAROD KINTZ

Skip to the end

In a segment on educational opportunity, BBC Radio 2 presenter Jeremy Vine received a phone call from a rather irate listener called Norman. Fit to burst by the time he finally got on air (his first words were 'Ah, at last!'), Norman seemed unable to get to the point.

During an incoherent diatribe that took in minute details from his early life, Norman told host Jeremy Vine not only to 'pipe down for a bit' but also to 'shut up, just shut up, please, and listen to me'. Having got no further in his argument Norman was finally ushered off air. Studio guest, motivational speaker Brad Burton, was perhaps a little generous when he said, 'Listen, Norman's entitled to his opinion.' While Jeremy Vine finished off the piece by voicing what all listeners had no doubt been thinking: 'I don't know what his opinion was.'

Oops, My Bad!

Yes, radio listeners can be lunatics. But sometimes the presenters aren't always that on the ball either.

Wrong number

While live on air, Australian DJ Rod Smith called up what he thought was the weather centre at Forest Hill, Melbourne. The idea for the segment was to give radio listeners an up-to-date weather report straight from the horse's mouth. Sadly, Smith mis-dialled . . .

Rod: Looks like we're in for a fine day?

Joe Public: I would think so.

Rod: What's it looking like your way?

Joe Public: Fine and sunny.

Rod: Going for a top twenty-three? What can you predict later on today, or through the week?

Joe Public: It will be a very sunny day. As you say, twenty-three.

Rod: And for Wednesday, would you say it's going to improve?

Joe Public: I have no idea.

Rod: [Laughs and hesitates.] . . . Well, with the weather it can change very quickly. Going for a top twenty-three . . . looking very good.

Joe Public: Looking lovely, been out for my walk this morning.

Rod: You guys at Forest Hill keep us up-to-date.

Joe Public: I hope we're not on air, Rod?

Rod: [Laughs, realizes he's in the shit.] Yes, we are.

Joe Public: You got the wrong number, mate.

FM breakfast show, Australia

'Radio is called a medium because it is rare that anything is well done.'

COMEDIAN FRED ALLEN

URBAN LEGENDS

The myths of live broadcast debunked

In August 1984, during his weekly radio address to the nation, Ronald Reagan was thought to have announced, 'My fellow Americans, I'm pleased to tell you today that I've signed legislation that will outlaw Russia for ever. We begin bombing in five minutes.'

However, Reagan did not in fact broadcast the bombing of Russia to a terrified wireless audience. According to reports he was known for regularly joking around prior to radio broadcasts. However, when the audio was leaked, the Russians were not amused.

CURRENT AFFAIRS

NEWSWORTHY GAFFES

Faced with a continuity error, some television presenters crumble. Panicking when forced to fill screen time without a script, they either stare blankly into the lens or verbally falter. But a rare few broadcasters manage to rise above the gaffes, as if nothing could ruffle their media-trained feathers. So this one's for you, Jeremy Paxman – we salute you, you sarcastic, unflappable bastard!

Accidents Happen

If you're in charge of a live broadcast the number one lesson to be learnt is: accidents can – and most probably will – happen.

'Here at Over Farm in Gloucester you're never short of things to look at and things to do. There are so many wonderful anima— [two enormous pigs are accidentally caught mating on camera] . . . er, haha!'

Unknown newscaster for a
UK local news report

'I can't hear a word. I don't know what's being said to me.'

Political broadcaster Robin Day,
proving live links are rarely a good idea

'...and if you're wondering what that noise was, it was my desk lamp falling over.'

Sarah Montague on Radio 4's *Today*
programme

Don't work with children, animals . . . or buses

A live broadcast in Cincinatti, Ohio, was interrupted in January 2012 when a bus almost mowed down a gathering of reporters. The assembled journalists were there for a press conference on, of all things, workplace safety, but were rudely interrupted when a bus barged into their throng. The vehicle's driver tried in vain to reverse her oversized chariot; when she couldn't she dismounted and gave the reporters a piece of her mind. Telling her attendant victims she was 'just trying to do her job', the lady bus driver added, 'If this group of people hadda moved out of the way, I wouldn't have ran into this truck!'

'The great thing about television is that if something important happens anywhere in the world, day or night, you can always change the channel.' AUTHOR UNKNOWN

Watch your back

Clocking the global trend for light-hearted news stories about cute animals, Saxony Zoo knew it was on to a good thing when it discovered Til, a bunny rabbit born without ears. A press conference was duly called in February 2012, but the rabbit's time in the spotlight was brief to say the least. During filming a cameraman took a wrong footing and stepped on the bunny, killing it instantly.

'I wish there was a knob on the TV so you could turn up the intelligence. They got one marked "brightness", but it don't work, does it.'

COMEDIAN LEO ANTHONY GALLAGHER

Naughty Newscasters

Those television professionals can be a cheeky, childish bunch, as these tales will attest.

Up yours!

A Russian news anchor raised her middle finger at President Obama when she thought the cameras weren't on her.

After reading out the US President's name during a news piece, loose-fingered Tatyana Limanova flipped up her middle finger in full view of the camera. Although she tried to claim her gesture had simply been 'a signal' to the autocue, the award-winning senior journalist was fired shortly after the incident.

Sleep easy

BBC News presenters are sometimes so bored by their programmes they fall asleep at their fancy news desk.

In March 2012, cameras panned onto fifty-year-old BBC *Breakfast* news presenter Simon McCoy when he had his head on the desk, apparently snoozing. Although McCoy later denied everything to his Twitter followers, saying, 'I was not asleep!', his co-host tweeted, 'Intravenous caffeine now being administered to @simonmccoy.'

Inveterate prankster

When he worked for Irish national network RTÉ, veteran broadcaster Terry Wogan used to burn his co-hosts' scripts while they were live on air.

Wogan admitted to it on the BBC's *Would I Lie to You?*, revealing that much of his early career involved quite a bit of pranking.

Jeremy Paxman:
Cross Him At Your Peril

Author, broadcaster, journalist, angry man: Jeremy Paxman tells it like it is.

'Good evening. If the autocue was working I could now read you something. But as it isn't, I can't.'

Jeremy Paxman, during the opening of BBC Two's *Newsnight*

'I'll be here again
tomorrow night, when
it would be jolly nice if
you could sit up and
pay attention.'

Jeremy Paxman, at the close of
Newsnight in 2008

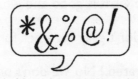

'…To tomorrow's weather
forecast. It's a veritable
smorgasbord! Sun! Rain!
Thunder! Hail! Snow!
Cold winds! It's almost
worth going to work.'

Jeremy Paxman:
sometime weather presenter

Paxman vs Blair

Getting up Tony's nose:

Paxman: Does the fact that George Bush and you are both Christians make it easier for you to view these conflicts in terms of good and evil?

Blair: I don't think so, no. I think that whether you're a Christian or not a Christian, you can try and perceive what is good and what is evil.

Paxman: You don't pray together, for example?

Blair: [Exasperated.] No, we don't pray together, Jeremy. No.

Newsnight, BBC Two

URBAN LEGENDS
The myths of live broadcast debunked

When NASA Space Shuttle *Challenger* undertook its tenth, disastrous, mission on 28 January 1986 it was thought to have been broadcast live by the BBC on children's programme *Newsround*.

However, although footage of the disaster – which resulted in the tragic death of all seven members of the crew – was shown during the opening titles, it had in fact occurred fifteen minutes earlier. *Newsround* was still the first to break the story and to broadcast the footage.

'Television has raised writing to a new low.'
SAMUEL GOLDWYN

Paxman vs his editor

Closing the show in the way only he knows how:

'That's all from *Newsnight* tonight. Martha's [Kearney] being punished for some offence in a previous life by presenting tomorrow's programme. In the meantime, it's all available again on our website, along with our editor's pathetic pleas for you to send some of us your old bits of home movie and the like so we can become the BBC's version of *Animal's Do the Funniest Things*. Good night.'

Newsnight, BBC Two

Paxman vs Blair, round two

Still getting up Tony's nose:

Blair: These are people who own the *Express* newspapers?

Paxman: Yes.

Blair: Right, well, in that case and in my view, it's perfectly acceptable for us to take a donation from them.

Paxman: They also own *Horny Housewives*, *Megaboobs*, *Posh Wives* and *Skinny and Wriggly*. Do you know what these magazines are like?

Blair: No.

Newsnight, BBC Two

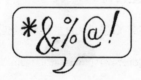

'Do I sometimes
set out to wrong-foot
people? Yes.'

Jeremy Paxman on his interviewing style

'And for tonight's
weather – it's April,
what do you expect?'

Jeremy Paxman at it again

Lessons in Newsreading

It's an important job that takes verve, intelligence and significant powers of concentration. If you're keen to take the plunge and become a newsreader, whatever you do, learn from the mistakes of these professionals.

1. Remember to pause

The script: This is *BBC World News*. I'm Jonathan Charles [PAUSE]. Kept hidden for almost two decades and forced to bear children . . .

How it was read by the newsreader: This is *BBC World News*. I'm Jonathan Charles, kept hidden for almost two decades and forced to bear children.

BBC World News

2. Try not to fumble your words

News host: Thank you very much, Rob. I'm back with a look at the head-weather . . . with the headlines . . . after a look at . . . the weather, with Rob McCowd . . . er . . . McCowdrey. Oh. God.

BBC World Service Television

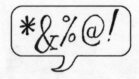

3. Do your homework

President Obama [after confirming the death of Osama bin Laden]: . . . May God bless the United States of America.

Fox News host: President Obama, speaking from the east room of the White House, telling us, the nation and *the world,* President Obama is, in fact, *dead.*

Fox 5 News

This wasn't the only time this happened – over fifty different TV hosts mixed up Osama's death with the death of the president.

4. Untie that tongue

News anchor: Prime Minister's Questions now
from Tony Black, Tony Blair, *back* with some
bleary-eyed nose ... er ... bleary-eyed news ...
I'm getting this all wrong, aren't I?

BBC *Six O'Clock News*

5. Read the script

The following exchange occurred on US television
during a traffic report that involved two unruly cows.

News anchor #1: Not many cars were moving, but
moo-ing could be heard on the Capital Beltway
around Washington, DC, earlier this morning.
A tractor-trailer transporting Black and Gus –
[one of the cows is shown on-screen] there's
Black or Gus – was stopped on the side of the
Beltway while the driver changed a flat tyre.

News anchor #2: [Sarcastically.] Wow, I wonder if those cows named Black and Gus were actually Black Angus cows, perhaps?

Anchor #1: Oh ... er, yes.

Anchor #2: You know, it's just a possibility.

Anchor #1: [Equally sarcastic.] Are you saying I misinterpreted something?

Anchor #2: No! [Gesturing to his co-host's script.] That was a government source, wasn't it?

[They both giggle.]

TECHNICAL GREMLINS

GHOSTS IN THE MACHINE

Irreverent subtitling, creative on-screen graphics, studios plunged into darkness during a broadcast: if there's going to be a technical spanner in the works, you can bet your bottom dollar it will happen live on TV.

Shonky Subtitles

The live broadcast might be going down without a hitch; the presenters delivering their lines with faultless aplomb; the guests behaving with complete decorum. But there's still room for error . . .

'Andy Murray has become Midge Ure.'

BBC Wimbledon coverage
(it should have read 'mature')

'The Chamber of horrors is starting to lurk.'

BBC News (it should have read, 'The Chamber of commerce is starting to help.')

'They love to nibble anything that comes into the shed, like our willies.'

BBC News during an outside broadcast with a pig farmer (who was wearing *wellies*)

'Well, that's twenty-two minutes Gordon Brown had the Queen in her private quarters.'

Sky News reporting on Gordon Brown's meeting *with* the Queen

'The Arch Bitch
of Canterbury.'

BBC News reporting on the baddest cleric in
Christendom

'The Clown is starting
to break, the skies are
starting to look Clare.'

BBC News reporting on the circus ...
I mean, the weather

'[The government] are making holes for surgeons.'

BBC subtitles that should have read 'making helpful decisions'

'I do not believe in soliciting myself.'

British broadcaster Andrew Neil on the BBC's *Daily Politics* (he actually said 'shortlisting')

'The Island rugby team.'

The BBC live subtitling system apparently does not care for *Irish* rugby players

'They will be toasted to their limits.'

Phillip Schofield describing the challenges facing the contestants on *Dancing On Ice*

'The sale of millions of puppies in Britain.'

BBC subtitles when covering Remembrance
Day – poppies, it seems, are so passé

'Engle Bert humper distinct.'

Engelbert Humperdinck, as announced by
subtitles on ITV1's *Loose Women*

'We will now have a moment's violence.'

BBC News 24 live subtitles, during the
Queen Mother's funeral in April 2002

'Mr Beryl Beryl.'

Live subtitles give Silvio Berlusconi, former
Prime Minister of Italy, a whole new name

'Jesus Christ.'

Live subtitling interpretation of 'GCHQ'
(Government Communications
Headquarters)

'There will be little silence
out of the Emirates today,
but both teams mock
the fact that tomorrow is
Remembrance Sunday.'

Match of the Day subtitling referring to a
football match at the Arsenal Emirates
Stadium – it should have read 'mark'

'"Very Super Tissues" – Stevie Wonder.'

BBC live subtitles, trying (but failing) to
indicate the use of Stevie Wonder's
'Superstition' lyric as background music

'Across the ice and
the Samaritans and
speedo you ... The
choreography for this
routine it's quite a
blasphemy ...
dolomite go horribly
one when you got
your Blades Court ...
I am begging you not
to dealers list.'

Subtitles on *Dancing on Ice*, which bought a
whole new meaning to the word 'baffling'.

Missing the Point

It might be a hard-rock number or a perhaps a heart-wrenching ballad, but whatever the tune chosen, background music is used to great effect by broadcasters to heighten the dramatic feel of a piece, or just to illustrate a point. But there have been times when the choice of music hasn't just been inappropriate, it's been downright offensive.

Not so precious

'Precious Things' by Tori Amos was used as backing music on a daytime antiques show, even though the song – and in fact the album – largely examines Amos's sexual assault as a young woman, feminism, and quite a lot of bleeding.

Built like a . . .

'Brick Shithouse' by Placebo was played over footage of rugby match highlights.

Gladys in da hood

In May 2010, during a CNN news report celebrating the fact that one-hundred-and-three-year-old pensioner Gladys Flamer was still able to drive herself around, the production team accidentally played the wrong music. As the tape of an elderly black woman rolled, rapper Coolio's 'Fantastic Voyage' accompanied the segment. With a lyric that included 'Everybody's got a stack and it ain't no crack,' poor Gladys's piece went down with some aplomb.

News anchor Kyra Phillips was later forced to apologize: 'It was the wrong music that aired, and we apologize for that. It was a terrible mistake, and we're working very hard to make up for that.'

A Gremlin in the System

During a repeat run of teleshopping programmes on the soon-to-be-defunct American cable channel Q2, the person in charge of the on-screen graphics was feeling a little naughty. Instead of backing-up the claims made by the presenter, the on-screen messages were anything but helpful. A lesson to television execs: this is what happens when you give a disgruntled, soon-to-be-let-go member of staff a little bit of last-minute freedom.

Polished off

Product advertised: 'Set of scratch remover tubes with polishing cloth (a snip at $19.00 with just $4.47 shipping and handling!)'

The accompanying on-screen graphics:
COMING UP: RICHARD SIMMONS . . . NAKED!!
JUST LIKE POLISHING A TURD . . .
THIRTY-DAY MONEY BACK GUARANTEE
NORMAL DELIVERY IS SEVEN TO TEN WORKING
DAYS
ALSO REMOVES WRINKLES AND LIVER SPOTS
I'M LONELY . . . CALL ME AT 610-701-8696
STILL LONELY . . . PLEASE CALL ME :-)
CAROLANN . . . GO INTO THE LIGHT!!!!!!!

'Television is now so desperately hungry
for material that they're scraping the top
of the barrel.   GORE VIDAL

Freedom from the kids

Product advertised: 'The Freedom Bag (a suitcase, at $33.00, down from $50.00!)'

Accompanying on-screen graphics: ADDED BONUS: POUCH TO STORE KIDS IN!

Neck on the line

Product advertised: 'Diane Young Coneflower Neckline Firmer $34.25'

Accompanying on-screen graphics:
MAY CAUSE CANCER THOUGH ...
I WONDER WHAT SHE'S THINKING RIGHT NOW
IS MY NECK REALLY THAT FAT????

'All television is children's television.'

RICHARD ADLER

You Can't Get the Staff!

Pity the poor newsreaders and presenters at the mercy of a sometimes dozy production team.

Unpaid bills

Colin Briggs (news anchor): Good morning. The accident and emergency unit in Newcastle now looks almost certain to move from its home in—

[The news studio lights turn off. The room is plunged into total darkness.]

Colin Briggs: Don't worry, we haven't paid the lighting bill.

[Poor Colin was forced to deliver the remainder of the news in silhouette.]

BBC local news

A bit of an earful

Faced with a revolving on-screen graphic and intro music that had stuck, this BBC News 24 presenter clearly had half the gallery shouting in her ear. Sadly, she opened the bulletin with:

News anchor: Good evening and welcome to the problem. We seem to be having some . . . a few problems this morning . . . I do apologize for that.

BBC News 24

Not my fault

News anchor: To autonomy, and onto the French
. . . National Assembly . . . has adopted . . . must
approve . . . the measures before . . . erm, a
constitutional review, ah, panel . . . I'm sorry,
this story is . . . absolute . . . erm . . . nonsense.
I'll continue with some headlines for you.

BBC World Report

I give up

'I really do apologize to both of you. It really is a complete shambles tonight.'

Jeremy Paxman, to his studio and
non-studio interviewees, during some
telephone-based trouble

Not right now

In 2009, football fans missed *the only goal* in the Merseyside FA Cup derby when ITV cut to the break during extra time. The last-minute goal meant Liverpool were knocked out of the cup, but both Everton and Liverpool fans failed to see it when an automated system (which controls when commercials are broadcast) overrode transmission of the game. Football fans were, understandably, rather furious.

The SHIT Awards

Other times it's the presenters *and* the production staff whose dozy antics lead to disaster. At the, now infamous, BRIT Awards in 1989, songwriting genius Mick Fleetwood and pint-size glamour model Samantha Fox delivered what has to be one of the worst presenting jobs in television history.

Although proceedings began well enough with a live performance from Gloria Estefan, it soon became apparent that the 5'1" Fox and 6'5" Fleetwood not only *looked* wrong on stage together, they also appeared monumentally uncomfortable presenting a live show. Indulging in some cringe-worthy ad-libbing and unable to hide the catalogue of continuity, technical and autocue errors that plagued the entire broadcast, Fleetwood and Fox also managed to announce the wrong winners *and* introduce the wrong guests.

The event was duly pre-recorded for the following eighteen years.

Steady Eddie

Sometimes it's the presenters, and not the production staff, who are responsible for the technical mishaps.

In 2010, during the presentation of a Samsung 50" HD-ready plasma TV on QVC in the UK, the presenter decided to show how hardy (he thought) the television was by punching it square in the screen.

Proclaiming that his nephew Hugh had 'put the hand controller from his wii straight through the screen of his LCD telly', the presenter, somewhat naively, added, 'you won't find that so much with a plasma TV'. After bashing his fist hard three times onto the TV, the sound of glass shattering could be heard, along with the presenters claim that, 'Oh, I've broken it . . . I think it's because I've done it so many times today.' I wonder how many of those TVs they managed to shift after that . . .

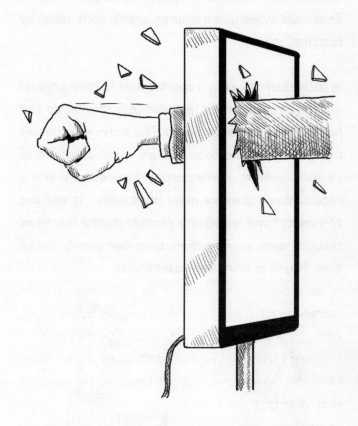

'Life doesn't imitate art, it imitates bad
television.'   WOODY ALLEN

A ghost in the machine

Sometimes it's difficult to point the finger of blame. Especially when the cameras aren't controlled by humans ...

A basketball report by a sportscaster in New England was interrupted when his newsdesk shuddered and began to emit strange noises. The noise was coming from a huge studio floor camera, which appeared to be moving of its own accord. It turned out it was a robotic camera with a mind of its own – it was out of control, and eventually ploughed into the news readers' desk, pushing them both completely out of shot. Maybe it didn't like basketball?

LANGUAGE PROBLEMS

MOUTH MALFUNCTIONS

Whether it's inadvertently letting a swear rip live on air, or getting their tongues tied up in knots, spare a thought for the presenters and newscasters who sometimes don't say what they mean.

Fluffing It Up

There's no chance of a second take during a live recording – bad news for the tongue-tied!

Malapropisms

Malapropism: n. Also, malaprop: 'The mistaken use of a word in place of a similar-sounding one, often with unintentionally amusing effect.' Such as:

> 'Ladies and gentlemen, we now bring you, from Salt Lake City, the famous Moron Tablenacker Choir.'
>
> Canadian radio announcer

'I don't know, man,
I might just fade into
Bolivian, you know
what I mean?'

Boxer Mike Tyson, speaking to reporters

'We cannot let
terrorists and rogue
nations hold this
nation hostile or hold
our allies hostile.'

George W. Bush

'This series has been
swings and pendulums
all the way through.'

Trevor Bailey, British cricket commentator

'He's going up and
down like a
metronome.'

Ron Pickering, BBC sports commentator

'Marie Scott … has
really plummeted to
the top.'

Alan Weeks, British sports commentator

'They have
miscalculated me as a
leader.'

George W. Bush

'Kerry is a lifeguard in her
local swimming pool …
she says weekends are
the worst – lots of
jumping in and bumming
all over the place.'

Newsreader Dominic Byrne on BBC Radio 1's
The Chris Moyle's Show

Spoonerisms

Spoonerism: n. Also, spoonerisms (plural): 'A verbal error in which a speaker accidentally transposes the initial sounds or letters of two or more words, often to humorous effect.' For example:

'Stifford Crapps'

Radio announcer McDonald Hobley,
introducing the British politician
Sir Stafford Cripps

'A shining wit.'

Comedian Barry Cryer on fellow
broadcaster Clive Anderson, on BBC Radio
4's *I'm Sorry, I Haven't a Clue*

'Rictoria Vagina.'

The *Antique Roadshow*'s ceramic expert David
Battie, trying to describe a piece of Victoria
Regina porcelain

'Masif Asood.'

Cricket commentator John Arlott on the
Pakistani fast bowler Asif Masood

'The next voice you'll
hear will be that of
our president,
Hoobert Heever.'

Radio announcer Harry von Zell,
commemorating the anniversary of President
Herbert Hoover's birth

Sporting Chance

Straight off the pitch with adrenaline pumping round their bodies, you could forgive sportsmen for committing the odd swearing-related gaffe – especially if they're faced with nosy journalists armed with a barrage of questions.

Quick off the mark

The bleepers weren't quick enough to mask the naughty language uttered by the following sportsmen.

'I'll have fucking sex tonight.'

An overexcited Peter Casey after a triumphant win at the horse races

Interviewer: 'You've achieved other things in your career. How does this compare?'

Wayne Rooney: 'Ah, it's the fucking best by far . . . [looks sheepishly at interviewer] sorry, ha, ha!'

Wayne Rooney, being interviewed live on
Sky Sports News

'Fucking wanker.'

Paul 'Gazza' Gascoigne, when the organizers
of the Italia '90 tournament asked each player
to mouth their name to camera for the
benefit of European TV stations

'My season was shit …
Can I say that?'

Football bad boy Mario Balotelli swears on
live TV after winning the FA Cup Final

FACT OF THE DAY

Theatre critic Kenneth Tynan was the first man to say 'fuck' on British television.

During a live BBC TV debate in 1965, Tynan was asked if he would ever consider staging a play that contained depictions of sexual intercourse. Tynan replied, 'I doubt if there are any rational people to whom the word fuck would be particularly diabolical, revolting or totally forbidden. I think that anything which can be printed or said can also be seen.'

Full blast

Lesson to all would-be journalists: Do not question legend Sir Alex Ferguson's leadership of Manchester United!

Geoff Shreeves: Had you ever known more pressure on you in your nineteen-year tenure?

Alex Ferguson: Nah, that's absolute bollocks, that.

Sky Sports News

A likely excuse

When Italian footballer Roberto Di Matteo uttered the word 'shit' live on Sky Sports, the kindly presenter immediately excused him because English is Di Matteo's second language: 'We're nearly past the watershed, but I know what you said. That's a word [former football manager] Dennis Wise taught him all those years ago – Dennis, it's your fault.'

Watch out!

While he was being interviewed for television at a football training session during his tenure as manager of Portsmouth Football Club, Harry Redknapp was hit by a football. He wasn't very happy about it.

Redknapp: We lost Festa with a ligament injury, he's having a scan today. I'm just hoping it's not as serious as we think it might be. So he's certainly

not going to be around. Arjan de Zeeuw's done a groin—

[Harry is hit by a football. He looks around, furious, for the culprit.]

Redknapp [to a player off camera]: WHY THE FUCK HAVE YOU KICKED THAT OVER HERE?

[The culprit can be heard trying to explain himself.]

Redknapp: WHAT? . . . YOU TRIED TO KICK IT IN THE GOAL AND YOU HIT ME? GOT SOME FUCKING BRAINS, HAVEN'T YOU? [Distracted and clearly still livid] No wonder he's in the fucking reserves.

The Ultimate Swear Word

It's a real divider, and no more so than when it's uttered on live television.

Too late!

These professionals have been known to let the odd one slip ...

'[After a video montage of Cantona] How cool is that! Great to see Eric C**t ... Cantona.'

BBC *Sportsday* host Olly Foster

'Cuts here, cuts there, cuts everywhere . . . Supposing, though, some of the people who *ought* to be paying taxes so the c**ts . . . cuts aren't so bad, aren't actually doing so.'

Jeremy Paxman on BBC Two's *Newsnight*, January 2011

'The roads and bridges
are closed and trains
in and out of the c**t
… county have been
cancelled.'

A Sky News presenter reporting on
flooding in Cornwall

'We've got a weather
c**t, er, front coming
down from Scotland.'

BBC weather presenter John Hammond

URBAN LEGENDS

The myths of live broadcast debunked

Although David Letterman's sidekick, band-leader Paul Shaffer, was thought to have been the first person to say 'fuck' on American television, it was in fact Grace Slick of rock group Jefferson Airplane.

The incident happened during the band's performance of 'We Can Be Together' on *The Dick Cavett Show* on 19 August 1969, the day after the legendary Woodstock concert. Slick refused to change the lyric 'Up against the wall, motherfucker'. In fact, she muttered the f-bomb twice during the performance.

Asking for it

If you're going to include a discussion on *The Vagina Monologues* on a live broadcast there's a fair chance the c-bomb might be dropped.

Jane Fonda: It wasn't that I wasn't a big fan. I hadn't seen the play, I live in Georgia . . . I was asked to do a monologue called 'C**t' . . . I said, I don't think so, I've got enough problems.

The Today Show, NBC, May 2008

'If it weren't for Philo T. Farnsworth, inventor of television, we'd still be eating frozen radio dinners.'

COMEDIAN JOHNNY CARSON

Serial offender

While discussing the thorny issue of fox hunting in April 2010, Radio 5 Live *Breakfast Show* host Nicky Campbell let one too many slip . . .

Nicky Campbell: Tim Bono from the Countryside Alliance – an organization which is, of course, pro-c**ting . . . er . . . hunting. Have you ever known a law so openly broken?

[Later in the show . . .]

Nicky Campbell: Georgie Worsley is master of the Old Surrey and Burstow and West C**t, Kent! Er, Hunt and is out hunting this morning in Lingfield in Surrey. Good morning.

Guest: Good morning to you. That was a bit of a slip of the tongue there!

Nicky Campbell: I know, I do apologize for that. It's very early in the morning and these things do happen and I do feel exceptionally embarrassed about it.

[Later still . . .]

Nicky Campbell: Lots of you are mentioning that they'll still be talking about the c**t, that, er, the West Kent Hunt that shall not be mentioned in five hundred years' time.

URBAN LEGENDS
The myths of live broadcast debunked

In July 1985, Sir Bob Geldof was thought to have said 'give us your fucking money' on live television as part of his fundraising efforts during the Live Aid broadcast.

However, Geldof actually said: 'Fuck the address, let's give the numbers' after the show's presenter asked Geldof to read out the address viewers could send their donations. According to reports, the public increased their donations significantly after Geldof's outburst, reaching a rate of £300 per second.

NAUGHTY, NAUGHTY

Behold! An impressive gathering of rebellious pop stars who've dared to utter swear words on live TV:

Hip-hop artist M.I.A. flipped up her middle finger during the Superbowl telecast in February 2012.

Ageing material girl Madonna shouted 'Come on, motherfuckers! Jump!' during the Live Earth broadcast in summer 2007.

Not to be outdone, Johnny Borrell of Razorlight fame dared to utter 'fuck' during the same Live Earth broadcast.

Serial award-winner Adele 'flipped the bird' (i.e. her middle finger) after accepting an award at 2012's BRIT Awards. Her speech was cut very short, which she clearly wasn't very happy about.

Jumping on the Live Earth swear-a-thon bandwagon, eighties legend Phil Collins *also* said 'fuck' while performing on stage.

Very naughtie

In December 2010, James Naughtie, veteran presenter of BBC Radio 4's very serious flagship breakfast show, the *Today* programme, came a cropper with Jeremy Hunt, the Culture Secretary. He lost the plot and it's a joy to hear.

James Naughtie: First up, after the news we're going to be talking to Jeremy C**t, er, Hunt, the culture secretary about [COUGH, suppressed giggle] broad . . . band. It's eight o'clock on Monday the sixth of December. [More suppressed giggles, coughs unconvincingly.] Er, sorry, terrible coughing fit.

[Later on in the show a helpful listener and psychology expert came to Naughtie's rescue . . .]

Evan Davis [co-host]: The prominent speech error in today's programme was more the Prime Minister's fault than Jim's, he says. 'It's well known in psycho-linguistic research that two words that share a vowel are prone to a speech error, in which initial consonants are exchanged. For this reason, making Jeremy Hunt the Culture Secretary was reckless in the extreme. Jim can be reassured, as can the listeners, that the underlying theory has far more explanatory value than Freud's theory of parapraxis, or Freudian Slips.'

Later that morning, on Andrew Marr's Radio 4 *Start the Week* programme:

Guest: We heard this morning one of the primary examples of the Freudian slip that we're ever likely to hear on Radio 4.

Andrew Marr: ...which we're not going to repeat ... Jeremy C**t, the, er, Hunt, the Culture Secretary had his name Freudianally transposed, er, as I've just done now ...

'If everyone demanded peace, instead of another television set, then there'd be peace.'   JOHN LENNON

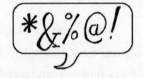

NIGHTMARE GUESTS

SACK THE CELEBRITY BOOKER

Television presenters don't always have it easy, especially when they're faced with a nightmare guest. Be it confronted with a prickly Hollywood starlet or an amorous puppet, at times like these the poor presenters have only one mantra: the show must go on!

Michael Parkinson: Where Angels Fear to Tread

Unafraid to ask awkward questions, the veteran broadcaster and journalist has managed to rile a few notable celebrities over the years.

Parkinson vs Meg Ryan

In October 2003, in one of TV land's most uncomfortable interviews, Parkinson, on his eponymous ITV chat show, conducted a fifteen-minute conversation of supreme awkwardness with Hollywood superstar Meg Ryan.

In a frosty exchange with a monosyllabic Ryan, Parkinson tried to probe the movie star about her comment that acting wasn't really in her nature, but she just wouldn't be drawn. Parkinson confronted Ryan about her wariness towards journalists – and to him in particular – before finding out she actually studied to be one prior to becoming an actor. Parky then asked her what she would do in his position as the conductor of the world's most awkward interview. Her response? 'Just wrap it up.' Which Parky duly did.

Ryan later said of Parkinson, 'I don't even know the man. That guy was like some disapproving father! It's crazy . . . he's a nut.' Meanwhile, Parkinson called the interview with Ryan his 'most difficult moment', adding, 'I should have closed it . . . She was an unhappy woman. I felt sorry for her. What I couldn't forgive her for was that she was rude to the other guests.'

Parkinson vs Helen Mirren

The grand dame of British acting talent, Helen Mirren, is as charming onscreen as she is off it. But early on in her career, a rather prickly Mirren took offence at Michael Parkinson's line of questioning during an interview on BBC1 in 1975.

Proceedings got off to a shaky start when Parky introduced Mirren using press quotes that variously described her as 'the sex queen of the Royal Shakespeare Company' and 'especially telling at projecting sluttish eroticism' – neither of which appeared to endear Mirren to him.

She then misunderstood him when he called her 'a serious actress' using air quotes (Mirren: 'In quotes? What do you mean, in quotes?'), and refused to play ball when he spent most of the interview trying to talk to her about her equipment (i.e. body), whereupon she (perhaps, understandably) came over a bit coy.

Parkinson vs Emu

This time it was Parkinson himself who got a bit riled. While interviewing popular entertainer Rod Hull and his puppet Emu on BBC 1 in 1976, poor Parky was faced with an overexcited bird . . .

In an encounter of increasing aggression, the puppet tried to overrule the poor presenter. After flooring Parky and throwing away one of his shoes, the bird then nipped the presenter on the arse. Parky finished the piece with, 'I knew I should never have booked you!'

Bird Brain

Parky wasn't the only celeb to face the relentlessly prodding beak of the puppet Emu.

Not in the script

In 1983, on ITV's *Good Morning Britain*, Emu tossed aside host John Stapleton and co-host Nick Owen's script, with pages flying all over the set. Emu could then be seen repeatedly nipping Owen's bottom for the entirety of the show's closing credits.

> 'I hate television. I hate it as much as peanuts. But I can stop eating peanuts.'
>
> ORSON WELLES

Brush with death

In 1981, on BBC 1's *Lena Zavaroni and Music*, the show's eponymous – and clearly terrified – star was forced to front a segment in which Rod Hull promised to demonstrate how to clean a pet bird with a brush. After asking Zavaroni to help scrub Emu's feet, Hull spent the majority of his appearance attempting to pin down the bird shouting, 'I've got him! Scrub his feet!' Alas, it was all a ruse, allowing Emu to grab the brush and clean Zavaroni's head with it.

Bad dog

In the 1990s, on Channel 4's hip TV show *The Word*, Emu took a special shine to the US gangster rapper Snoop Doggy Dogg. The hip-hop star patted the bird's head politely at first, but all hell broke loose when host Mark Lamarr produced his own (rather mean and considerably larger puppet) and began to attack another guest. Amidst the chaos, Snoop could be seen pushing Emu away, before trying to rip his head off. Lamarr then asked Snoop, 'Do you have anything like this on TV shows in America?' Snoop said absolutely nothing.

Who Let *Them* On?

The annals of television are packed full of irate presenters and slightly mad guests . . .

Speak up!

In 1983, on Channel 4's *Loose Talk*, in what's reported to be his first appearance on television, *Private Eye* editor Ian Hislop managed to clash with no less a figure than rock's most famous, gravelly voiced troubadour, Tom Waits. The problem was, Hislop didn't think Tom was talking loud enough.

Hislop later said of his first foray into television interviewing: 'I had to talk to a man called Tom Waits, who had flown in and had what was called "jet lag" – as celebrities call it. I think he'd put a huge amount of jet lag up his nose.'

Here's how the awkward exchange went down:

Tom Waits [haltingly, and very quietly]:   Part of the reason I'm here is that I have a new piece of work that's out . . .

[An uncomfortable silence.]

Ian Hislop: Can I suggest you plug it a bit louder? I mean, if that's what you're over here for.

Waits: I'll plug it my own damn way, you know?

Hislop: It's just very soft.

Waits: Well, I think you can hear me, can't you?

Hislop: Yeah, but I'm fairly near.

[At this point, Hislop simply turned in his seat and looked, baffled, at the three other guests – all three of whom failed to rescue him.]

> 'Television is not real life. In real life people actually have to leave the coffee shop and go to jobs.' BILL GATES

The Cruisenator

In what would turn out to be one of his most explosive appearances ever (and that includes his performance on Oprah's sofa), Tom Cruise was invited to talk to Matt Lauer on NBC's *Today Show* in 2005 about psychiatry and anti-depressants.

Overusing the host's name (his sentences were punctuated by a chorus of 'Matt, Matt, Matt'), Cruise waxed lyrical about his thoughts on actress Brooke Shields's choice to take antidepressants to treat post-natal depression. His comments included the following crackers:

- I've never agreed with psychiatry . . . It's a pseudo-science.

- Do you know now that Ritalin is a street drug? Do you understand that?

- You don't know the history of psychiatry. I do.

- There is no such thing as a chemical imbalance.

- [To the host] You're glib. You don't even know what Ritalin is.

Stick to making films, Tom!

Keep going . . .

In December 1976, the Sex Pistols made a now infamous appearance on Bill Grundy's magazine show. And what a strange beast it was – as belligerent as the Pistols' behaviour was, it's hard not to feel more blame lies with veteran broadcaster Bill Grundy. He wanted them to drop the f-bomb; he seemed to *goad* them.

Grundy: Now I want to know, are you serious about what you're doing?

Glen Matlock [bassist]: Oh, yeah.

Grundy: Beethoven, Mozart, Bach, Brahms ...

Johnny Rotten [singer]: They're all heroes of ours, ain't they? [sarcastically] They're *wonderful* people. They really turn us on.

Grundy: Well suppose they turn other people on?

Rotten [quietly]: That's just their tough shit.

Grundy: It's what?

Rotten: Nothing. A rude word. Next question.

Grundy: No, no, what was the rude word?

Rotten: Shit.

Grundy: Was it really? Good heavens, you frighten me to death. What about you girls, behind?

Matlock: He's like your dad, ain't he, this geezer? . . . Or your grandad.

Grundy [to Siouxsie Sioux]: Are you worried, or are you just enjoying yourself?

Siouxsie Sioux: Enjoying myself . . . I've always wanted to meet you.

Grundy: We'll meet afterwards, shall we?

Steve Jones [guitarist]: You dirty sod. You dirty old man!

Grundy: Well keep going, chief, keep going. Go on, you've got another five seconds. Say something outrageous.

Jones: You dirty bastard!

Grundy: Go on, again.

Jones: You dirty fucker!

Grundy: What a clever boy!

Jones: What a fucking rotter.

The wrong guest

Poor Guy Goma. All he did on 8 May 2006 was turn up on time to a job interview at BBC Television Centre. The last thing the IT specialist expected was to be picked up mistakenly from reception by a member of the BBC News 24 production team, who should have in fact collected Guy Kewney, a respected technology journalist who was due to talk on air about online music piracy. Guy Goma duly appeared on screen, and, ever the sport, ably mucked in and tried to answer anchor Karen Bowerman's questions, even though they'd, quite literally, got the wrong Guy.

Bowerman: Well, Guy Kewney is editor of the technology website News Wireless. [Camera flashes to Guy, whose face wears a look of confusion and horror.] Hello, good morning to you.

Goma: Uh, good morning?

Bowerman: Were you surprised by this verdict today?

Goma: I am very surprised to see this verdict because I was not expecting that. When I came, they told me, 'You've got an interview' and that's all. So it's a big surprise.

Bowerman: With regards to the costs involved, do you think now more people will be downloading online?

Goma: Actually, you're going to see a lot of people downloading from the Internet. But I think it is much better for the development to inform people what they want.

Bowerman: This does really seem to be the way the music industry's progressing now, that people want to go onto the website and download music.

Goma: Exactly. It is going to be an easy way for everyone to get something from the Internet.

Bowerman: Guy Kewney, thanks very much indeed.

In your face!

In 2007, while being interviewed in the player tunnel after a victorious match against West Bromwich Albion, Stephen Bywater – serial-TV-prankster (he once spelled out the c-word on live TV) and former goal-keeper for Derby County – was attacked from all angles by his fellow players.

Heroically maintaining his decorum as he responded to the interviewer's questions, Stephen was targeted with a series of pranks, including having his shirt pulled over his head, his hair ruffled, a kiss planted on his cheek, hands in his face, and, finally, talcum powder rubbed into his face.

Best of Friends

People – presenters and guests included – should of course be on their best behaviour when appearing on live TV. But it seems the bright lights and certain tensions bubbling under the surface can sometimes lead to explosive on-screen encounters . . .

Brace yourself . . .

In 1982, comedian Andy Kaufman and wrestler Jerry 'The King' Lawler's appearance on *Late Night with David Letterman* ended in tears. Specifically Kaufman's. Kaufman was asked by Letterman if the public feud between the two men was genuine, after they had fought a wrestling bout that appeared to have left Kaufman in a neck brace – which he was still sporting.

Lawler immediately retorted with, 'No, not at all. I couldn't warm up to this guy if we were cremated together. No. Matter of fact, he is a wimp.' After a brief and heated exchange between the two men, Lawler stood up, hoicked up his waistband and backhanded Kaufman right across the head. The house band began to play, the show cut to a quick break, but events didn't end there . . .

After the break, Kaufman reappearsed onstage and, from behind the safety of Letterman's desk, let rip at Lawler:

'I am sick of this bullSHIT! You are full of bullshit, my friend! I will sue you for everything you have! I will sue your ass! You're a motherfucking ASSHOLE! You hear me! A fucking asshole! FUCK YOU! I will get you for this! . . . I am sorry! I am sorry to use those words on television! I apologize. But you, you're a FUCKING ASSHOLE! [Jumps up and down.] A FUCKING ASSHOLE! You HEAR ME?! A FUCKING ASSHOLE!

He then grabbed Letterman's coffee from his desk and threw it over Lawler, who leaped out of his chair. Kaufman, quite wisely, made a very quick exit.

Chief Whippers

Politicians, it seems, fair no better in the on-screen spat stakes.

Your mum smells!

Verbal clashes on news programmes have nothing on the fracas that occurred live on Lebanese television in November 2011. During a debate between the leader of the Ba'ath Party, Fayez Shukur, and ex-MP Mustafa Alloush, what began as a heated debate between political rivals quickly turned nasty – with Alloush calling Shukur a 'tyrant', 'criminal' and 'liar'.

Shukur soon retaliated by insulting Alloush's mother and throwing his pen and a cup of water at him. As the two guests sprung out of their seats, the show's host was forced to intervene and stop them from physically coming to blows – although by that time, Shukur had picked up his chair, ready to throw it.

Both parties refused to leave the show and, after ten minutes off air, they simply resumed the broadcast and the debate, which then passed off without incident.

WEATHERMEN

IT'S RAINING DIVAS

Weathermen and -women are often seen as harmless televisual types, called upon to smile even when they're telling us it's going to rain all summer. But there is a surprisingly naughty streak in the ranks of meteorology. All these stories have left me wondering whether giggling, doing finger swears and having on-camera strops are not so much faults but requirements for the job.

Tomasz Schafernaker: Weather Bad Boy

Tomasz Schafernaker is a BBC weatherman come poster-boy, who has posed, in his pants, for a men's magazine (he's actually got an eight-pack). On top of that, he has committed at least three, priceless, live TV blunders.

Strike ONE!: the diva strop

Caught unaware when the camera came to the weather studio before he was ready, Tomasz simply stood there silently as the BBC weather ident blared behind him. Realizing he was on camera, Tomasz simply scowled and said, 'I don't know if I'm on camera or not!' He then removed his microphone, unloosened his fetching pink tie, and walked off set. Weather Diva!

'[Television is] the triumph of machine over people.' COMEDIAN FRED ALLEN

Strike TWO!: Glastonbury

Reading the weather live on Radio 4's flagship *Today* programme, Tomasz was reporting from the often-boggy environs of the Glastonbury Festival. Ever the professional, Tomasz delivered a note-perfect bulletin. Well, at least until he reached the part about rain. According to the script, he was meant to describe how a forecast bad spell was likely to turn the festival into a 'muddy site'. Alas, he used instead the rather unfortunate 'muddy shite,' and then collapsed, giggling his way through the rest of the broadcast like a schoolboy.

Strike THREE!: finger swears

An insight into the bantering atmosphere of the BBC News studio was glimpsed when Tomasz was introduced by a (rather sarcastic) Simon McCoy. Newsreader McCoy began by saying, 'Now we'll have the weather forecast in just a minute. Of course it will be 100 per cent accurate and provide you with all the details you could possibly want.' Cue Tomasz, who decided to gesture at McCoy with his middle finger, using the universal hand gesture for 'jog on'. Despite trying to disguise the hand signal as a chin scratch, viewers were not fooled. Neither was fellow broadcaster Fiona Armstrong, who let out a thoroughly lady-like, 'Oh!'

'When television is good, nothing is better. When it's bad, nothing is worse.'

FORMER CHAIRMAN OF THE
FEDERAL COMMUNICATIONS COMMISSION,
NEWTON N. MINOW

Storms Ahead

Whatever the weather, you'd be forgiven for expecting the forecast to be delivered with grace, poise and professionalism. Think again.

Watch your back

In February 2010, Steve Jacobs, a weatherman for Australia's Channel Nine, presented a weather bulletin from inside the pelican pen at Taronga Zoo. As Jacobs began his broadcast, one of the pelicans soon proved just how friendly he was, and Jacobs could be heard shouting, 'AAAAAAARGH! My arse! My arse!' Jacobs was forced to abandon his bulletin as the pelican pecked at him affectionately.

'Television is like the American toaster: you push the button and the same thing pops up every time.'   ALFRED HITCHCOCK

Fifteen minutes of fame

This weathergirl on WVTM, in Alabama, USA, showed the news anchor who's boss.

Weathergirl: 62 degrees tonight, and you'll notice the rain and storms arrive tomorrow, mainly during the afterno—

[Female news anchor takes wrong turn and strides in front of weather graphic.]

Weathergirl [to anchor]: Wait your turn, Brooke, wait your turn.

'Radio is the theatre of the mind; television
is the theatre of the mindless.'
TELEVISION PERSONALITY STEVE ALLEN

Mind your ps and qs

In February 2012, BBC weatherman Alex Deakin did the unimaginable . . .

Alex Deakin: . . . Some towns and cities may just stay a squeak above zero but it's going to be a cold start to Sunday and while we've got the showers that obviously does bring the risk of some ice on the roads through the night and into Sunday morning. By and large though it is, simply, a lovely winter's day tomorrow. Bucket loads of c**t, of, er, of sunshine in central and eastern areas. Some showers will continue across northern areas.

Alex Deakin later tweeted: 'I think the less said the better about that last broadcast #P45.'

High winds

'... And then we should see a lot of sunshine across many parts of the country, a much better day than it's been today. Cloud will increase from the west [emits a loud burp] ... ooh, sorry, a bit of wind there, too.'

BBC News weatherman

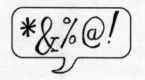

SOURCES

actiononhearingloss.org.uk
alphadictionary.com
bbc.co.uk
blogbaladi.com
books.google.co.uk
break.com
channel4.com
charlieswinbourne.com
chm.bris.ac.uk
dailymail.co.uk
dailyrecord.co.uk
dangerousminds.net
dvdfever.co.uk
everything2.com
freakipedia.net
guardian.co.uk
herald.ie
huffingtonpost.com
iannoon.wordpress.com
imdb.com
independent.co.uk
itv.com
jimromenesko.com
kontraband.com
maciverblog.co.uk
mediaite.com
mentalfloss.com
metro.co.uk

mirrorfootball.co.uk
monsterkidclassichorrorforum.
   yuku.com
naharnet.com
news.sky.com
nytimes.com
oddee.com
onemansblog.com
onthisfootballday.com
otrsportsonline.com
paulgoodman67.hubpages.com
pbh2.com
radio.about.com
radiovoxpopuli.org
scotsman.com
seniorlivingmag.com
snopes.com
speedyshare.com
telegraph.co.uk
theblaze.com
thesun.co.uk
thewestmorlandgazette.co.uk
thinkexist.com
usmagazine.com
wikipedia.org
youcantmakeitup.blogspot.co.uk
youtube.com

Also available from **Michael O'Mara Books**
priced at **£7.99**

Man Fail
by Marion Appleby
ISBN: 978-1-84317-698-5

Universally Challenged
by Wendy Roby
ISBN: 978-1-84317-466-0